DENMARK GETS THE NEWS OF '76

Denmark
Gets the News of '76

BY THORKILD KJÆRGAARD

DANISH BICENTENNIAL COMMITTEE

COPENHAGEN

1975

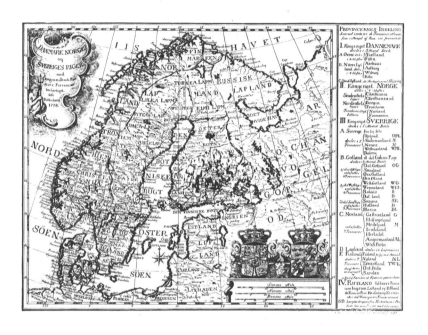

Danish map of 1778 of the Scandinavian kingdoms.
The Royal Library, Copenhagen.

4

Denmark in 1776

In addition to present-day Denmark (including the Faroe Islands and Greenland), the Danish states in 1776 embraced Norway, the Dukedoms of Schleswig and Holstein to the south, as well as Iceland and some lesser overseas possessions, such as the three West Indian islands of St. Croix, St. Thomas, and St. John. These Virgin Islands were later sold to the United States.

The combined population in these areas was about 2,250,000, of which 800,000 lived within the present-day borders of the Kingdom of Denmark.

Denmark was an agricultural society, and up to 90 per cent of the population lived on the land. The capital of Copenhagen, with its more than 80,000 inhabitants, by the power of its size alone was superior to any other town in the realm. Copenhagen was more than four times larger than the next largest city, Altona, in Holstein, while Odense, the largest provincial town inside the borders of present-day Denmark, numbered only slightly over 5,000 inhabitants.

The language in the central parts of the realm was Danish. In Holstein and parts of Schleswig, German was the everyday tongue.

In accord with the Danish Royal Law of 1665, political power rested without restriction with the sovereign monarch – who in practice, however, exercised his authority through an all-embracing and dependable bureaucracy.

Denmark was not then one of the great European powers, but by virtue of its considerable size and its position at the entrance of the Baltic, the country was far from a negligible quantity in the European world.

This forever memorable day

By Karl Skytte

The American Declaration of Independence, which was signed in Philadelphia on July 4, 1776, marked the advent of momentous political developments on the North American continent and in Europe. The Declaration did not only lay the foundation of a democratic constitution for the United States; it also became the source of inspiration for the political upheavals in the Old World from which emerged, in the eighteenth and nineteenth centuries, the dedication of the countries of Western Europe to democratic rule, human rights and fundamental freedoms. The ideology of the Declaration was deeply rooted in European thought, and outmoded authoritarian forms of government ripened Europe for responsiveness to the message from Philadelphia. On that score, the Declaration of Independence had a decisive impact on the course of events leading to the attainment, in 1849, of Denmark's first democratic constitution.

The history of the twentieth century has shown that the idea of government for the people and by the people has not won universal acceptance; this idea remains a matter of paramount concern. Only by persistent and vigilant efforts to develop and improve the system of democratic rule, and only by unity and solidarity among the states dedicated to the ideals of democracy, shall we be able to preserve the values enshrined in the American Declaration of Independence.

The Danish Government has accorded me the honor of appointing me President of the Danish Bicentennial Committee which is entrusted with the task of preparing and carrying out Danish activities in celebration of the Bicentenary of the American Declaration of Independence. One of the projects is this book, which the Committee asked Thorkild Kjærgaard, M.A., of the University of Copenhagen, to write.

The book tells how the news of the Declaration was received in Denmark and analyzes the impact of the Declaration on public

7

opinion in different strata of Danish society in the 1770s and Denmark's attitude toward America in those turbulent years. Mr. Kjærgaard takes up a subject never before treated in literature: the question of what impression the young United States of America made on the oldest kingdom of Europe.

One of the first Europeans to analyze the relationship of political developments in America and Europe was the Danish civil servant C. F. von Schmidt-Phiseldeck, who in 1820 published a farsighted book entitled *Europe and America*. The author's characterization of the Fourth of July 1776 as "this forever memorable day" testifies to his clear vision of the abiding significance of the Declaration of Independence.

Karl Skytte is president of the Danish Parliament and chairman of the Danish Bicentennial Committee.

On July 2, 1776, the Second Continental Congress, assembled in Philadelphia, declared the thirteen American colonies to be independent of Great Britain. Two days later, on July 4, 1776, the delegates explained in the Declaration of Independence to "a candid World" why the patriots had decided to free themselves from the British Parliament and the British people.

The aim of the Declaration was to foster an understanding of the American action, not least in Europe, where a sensitive public eagerly followed the events from the remote front across the Atlantic.

Meanwhile, two months were to pass before even a modest segment of the population of the Kingdom of Denmark in northern Europe, where King Christian VII had reigned as absolute monarch since 1766, learned of the Continental Congress's epochal "Declaration."

These were the subjects who read the country's largest newspaper, *De til Forsendelse med Posten allene privilegerede Kiøbenhavnske Tidender* [*The solely privileged for Dispatch by the Post Copenhagen Times*], (1) issued twice weekly in the capital of Copenhagen, with a circulation of under 3,000. (2) On Tuesday, September 2, 1776, this paper published an edited excerpt from the Declaration of Independence on its front page. Now on that day, and the days that followed, as *Kiøbenhavnske Tidender* gradually reached its subscribers in Copenhagen and the provinces, these subjects had a chance to gain some acquaintance with the famous text – about which, before that day, only a small circle around the government and the readers of various foreign language newspapers had been informed, and then only for a very few days. The Department of Foreign Affairs first received the announcement of American independence on August 30 in a depèche from the government's diplomatic envoy in London, Frederik von Hanneken.

The Declaration of Independence, which for many in the old European states arrived like a torch of freedom from the other side

Ao. 1776.   **No. 71.**

De   til
Forsendelse   med Posten
allene   privilegerede
Kiøbenhavnske   Tidender.

Mandagen, den 2den September.

Af disse Tidender udgives ugentlig 2de Stykker, ved Brødrene Johan Christian og Georg Christopher Berling.

London, den 16de Aug.

Efter en Afskrivt, som man har her om General Congressens Erklæring af 4de Julii, hvorved deh erk [de] ere de foreenede Colonier for en frie og uafhængig Stat, indeholdes derudi fornemmeligt følgende: Naar det i det menneskelige Tildragelsers Løb, er for et Folk nødvendigt, at sønderrive de Stats-Baand, hvorved det er foreenet med et andet Folk, og iblandt Jordens Magter at antage, den afsondrede og lige Rang, hvortil Naturens Lov og Gud selv har forlenet det Ret, saa fordrer en anstændig Ærbødighed, for den menneskelige Tænkemaade, offentlig at legge Verden for Øyne, de Grunde, som bevæge samme Folk til denne Afsondring. Vi holde det og for sig selv disse Sandheder noksom beviiste, at alle Mennesker ere eens skabte, at de af Skaberen ere blevne begavede med visse ubetalige Rettigheder, iblant hvilke henhøre Liv, Frihed og Ret til at befordre sin egen Lykke; at der, for at være forsikkret om disse Rettigheder, ere blevne oprettede Regieringer iblandt Menneskerne, som have deres retmæssige Magt af deres Bifald, som blive regierede; og at Folket, naar en Regieringsform strider mod denne Hensigt, har Ret til at forandre eller tilintetgiøre den, og derimod at oprette en nye Regiering, grunde den saaledes, og indrette dens væsentlige Styrke saaledes, som det paa bedste Maade kan synes at befordre sin Roe og Velfærdt. Forsigtighed lærer vel, at længe befæstede Regieringer ikke bør forandres formedelst smaa og hastige Aarsager; og Erfarenhed har ogsaa lært, at Menneskeligheden er meere tilbøyelig til at taale, saalænge den taales, end forskaffe sig selv Ret med at forandre Regieringsformen, som den er vant til. Men, naar mangfoldige Uheld og uretmæssige Anmasselser, uophørlig modstride benævnte Hensigt, og Øyemærket beviser, at det sigter til at bringe Folket under en fuldkommen Despotismum, da er det samme Folks Ret, ja Pligt at afkaste slig en Regiering, og forsyne sig med nye Beskiermere for sin tilkommende Sikkerhed. Saaledes har disse Coloniers Taalmodighed været, og saaledes forholder det sig med Nødvendigheden, som tvinger dem til at forandre Regieringsformen. Historien af de nu værende i Storbrittanien, er en Historie af igientagne Fornærmelser og uretmæssige Afpresselser, som have intet andet Øyemeed havt, end ... i disse Lande at befæste. Til Beviis herpaa, blive disse Begivenheder forelagte en upartisk Verden. Efter en vidtløftig Fortælling af igientagne Besværelser, som de forgiæves have bragt for Kongen, for Parlementet, for Nationen, ende de Erklæringen med disse Ord: Desaarsag Vi, Repræsentanterne af de foreenede Stater i America forsamlede i en General-Congres, formedelst vores Tænkemaades Oprigtighed beraabe os paa den allerhøyeste Verdens Dommere, og af Kraft og i det forsamlede gode Folks Navn i disse Colonier, giøre hermed høytidelig bekiendt og erklære: At disse foreenede Colonier ere og bør med Ret være frie og uafhængige Stater; at de afsige sig fra al Lydighed imod den Brittiske Krone, og at alle Statsbaand og Forbindelser imellem dem og Staten af Storbrittanien, ere og skal være ganske tilintetgiorte, at de derfor som frie og uafhængige Stater, have den fuldkomneste Ret og Magt, at føre Krig, og giøre Fred, slutte Forbindelser og indgaae Alliancer, befæste Reglementer i Hensigt til Handelen, og overhovedet, at foretage alt, hvad uafhængige Stater paa en Lovformig Maade kan giøre. I fast Tillid til det Guddommelige Forsyns Beskiermelse, forbinde vi os med hverandre, at befæste denne Erklæring med vort Liv, med vort Gods og med vor Ære.

Underskrevet, paa Befaling og i Congressens Navn den 4de Julii 1776.

John Hancock, Præsident. Hr. Thomson, Secretarius.

Man har paalidelige Efterretning om at Congressen har oprettet en Militairisk Orden, som skal opmuntre Provincial-Officeererne til Tapperhed. Samme skal kaldes Independents Ordenen. Den bestaaer af Congressens Præsident John Hancock og 24 andre Riddere, hvoriblant Generalerne Washington, Putnam og Wooster ere. Ordenstegnet er en femkantet Sølv-Stierne paa Brystet og et Løsegrønt Baand over den høyre Skulder, med en Figur af America,

Front page of Kiøbenhavnske Tidender (The Copenhagen Times), September 2, 1776, the date that an edited excerpt from the Declaration of Independence appeared for the first time in Danish.

of the ocean, was tossed into the population of perhaps the most peaceful and well-rooted of all the absolute monarchies in Europe: the Kingdom of Denmark. What happened then?

What news was fit to print?

One can imagine how editorial judgement at Denmark's leading newspaper must have been taxed over how to handle the sensational Declaration from Philadelphia. The problem was twofold. First, no one could be sure that the text was authentic. There were several instances from the American War of Independence of false news being deliberately circulated. In fact, just before the Declaration reached Europe, newspapers in northern Germany, as well as *Kiøbenhavnske Tidender*, had warned against the propagation of false news. This problem does not appear to have been decisive for the Danish press. But it is worth noting that one distinguished German journal, the extremely reliable *Reichs-Post-Reuter* of Hamburg, did not print the Declaration, ostensibly because the paper had information from London that the document was an English falsification! (3) Whatever their reasons, a number of other German papers did not print it, either.

Far more important was the question of how much of the news was deemed fit to print. Though there was no prepublication censorship of the press in Denmark in 1776, there still were limits to what could be published. Newspapers were forbidden "to introduce anything...which relates to the State and the Government,...[and] which contains anything offensive, or Improper..." under a Royal Ordinance of October 20, 1773. This stipulation was hazy and forced the press to tread softly. For who could know ahead of time what, in specific instances, would be considered "offensive" or "Improper," and whether the Declaration of Independence might so be considered?

Quite clearly, the document contained nothing about the Danish King or the kingdom he ruled. Yet it spelled out clearly a number of political maxims which lay far from those on which the Danish monarchy rested. Not least, it leveled a scorching attack on the British King George III, who happened to be one of the Danish King's most powerful colleagues. There also may have been the fear that foreign diplomats, who had a habit of delving into newspapers after passages that could be construed as offensive to their countries, would object to seeing the Declaration of Independence in print.

It must have been a delicate subject to approach. A closer look at the different versions published in the Danish realm allows one to draw certain inferences about the decisions made. As will be seen, great pains were taken to avoid directly disparaging statements about the British monarch, and thereby about monarchs in general. Yet there seems to have been no compulsion to suppress radical democratic ideas, even though, in principle, they were far removed from the ideological precepts of the Danish monarchy.

With this in mind, it is understandable that all the Declaration's introductory paragraphs could be printed uncut up to the sentence, "The history of the present King of Great Britain is a History of repeated Injuries and Usurpations, all having in direct object the Establishment of an absolute Tyranny over these States." That sentence presumably was *not* fit to print in the Kingdom of Denmark. In any event, it was edited by *Altonaischer Mercurius* [The Altona Mercury], published in Altona, Holstein, where the Danish King ruled as a duke. In this paper's German version of the Declaration, which formed the basis of the first Danish translation in *Kiøbenhavnske Tidender,* the words "King" and "of absolute Tyranny" were simply omitted, so that the sentence in German, and accordingly the first version in Danish, become completely confused. Translating directly from the Danish:

"The history of the present of Great Britain is a History of repeated Injuries and Usurpations which have had no Purpose other than...to establish in these States."

Regarding the Declaration's grievances, which attribute to the British sovereign a decisive personal responsibility for the course of events, and thereby level direct attacks on the monarch's person, *Altonaischer Mercurius* solved the problem elegantly by publishing the document in two parts. The grievances appeared alone in part two. Who the constantly referred to *Er* (He) – that is, the King – was, never was mentioned (but could possibly be guessed). In Copenhagen, *Kiøbenhavnske Tidender* preferred not to print the grievances in its first release. Later, in October, when the paper ran the only coherent and reasonably complete Danish version known from that time, direct references to the Crown still were deleted, so the sense of the text was significantly altered. Instead, for every mention of "the King" in the original document, "the Ministry" (in other words, the British Ministry) was inserted in the October Danish version. Where the Declaration tended, hardly with justification, to charge George III with almost total responsibility for the course of events

Christian VII (1749–1808), King of Denmark in 1766–1808. Painting by Jens Juel, 1787. Rosenborg Collection.

leading up to July, 1776, (4) the Danish edition laid all the responsibility on the British Ministry, and the king was never even named. How these small alterations changed the color of the Declaration can be seen in the edited sentence as it appeared in the extended Danish version in October, 1776. Again translating from the Danish, it now reads:

"The History of the present State of the Ministry in Great Britain is a History of frequently occurring Affronts, and wrongful Oppressions, all of which have aimed at the establishment in these Countries of an absolute Tyranny."

Direct interference with the press in those days was rare in Denmark. It has been suggested that, among other things, this was due to a "quiet censorship" – meaning that the writers and publishers themselves, with their rewrites, camouflages, and ommissions, displayed something less than candidness in what they published. (5) There is no way to assess the effects of such quiet censorship on the press and cultural life as a whole in this period. It simply operated too subtly! In the case of the various translations and editions of the Declaration of Independence, however, we have a bold and illustrative example of "quiet censorship" in action. One senses the pressure that newspaper publishers and writers were up against: they had to be very careful about the fitness of the news they printed.

Even so, the press and other publications still enjoyed significant freedom of action, since in its real essentials, the radical document *was* published in Denmark's largest newspaper without legal retaliation by the government. In other words, no insurmountable obstacles were raised by Denmark's ruling authorities to prevent modern political opinions from being brought to public attention.

From Philadelphia to Danish newspaper readers

But why, then, did it take sixty days from the time the Declaration was issued in Philadelphia to the time it could be read in Danish in Copenhagen? As an account of the document's difficult journey to Denmark will show, the explanation lay above all in the fact that, seen through modern eyes, news transmission over long distances in those days, like all forms of transportation at the end of the eighteenth century, was slow and full of detours.

Immediately after the Declaration was ratified, copies were shipped off to several European states. But since it took so long to sail from America to Europe, normally not less than four weeks, (6) there was

An 1817 Danish school map of America. Denmark appears in the upper right corner. The three Danish West Indian islands are inset in a frame at the lower left. The Royal Library, Copenhagen.

15

Danish postal rider from the time of Christian VII. Front page vignette from the newspaper, Den Kongelige Maanetlige Post Rytter (The Royal Monthly Postal Rider).

bound to be a long delay before the text was published in a Europe where papers everywhere, including Denmark, long had been full of rumors about the intentions of the Continental Congress.

Not until mid-August was the manifesto generally known in Great Britain via the London newspapers. (7) The same papers carried transcripts of the famed statement further eastward, presumably via the regular postal route over Cuxhaven to the region of Hamburg, where for years the press had occupied a key position as agent of the news from southern and western foreign areas to Scandinavia, not least Denmark, whose southern border stretched all the way down to Hamburg. Knowledge of German was taken for granted among educated Danes, and scholarly works often were published in German.

About a week after the Declaration had become known in London, it appeared in Hamburg area newspapers. *Staats- und Gelehrte Zeitung des Hamburgischen unpartheyischen Correspondenten* [State- and Learned Times of the Hamburger nonpartisan Correspondent] published a German translation, although with the grievances omitted, for its readers on August 24. And as mentioned, *Altonaischer Mercurius* printed the text in its entirety, although with references to "the King" deleted, and in two parts, so that the complaints appeared alone. These were the issues of August 23 and 26, 1776 (numbers 136 and 137).

Altonaischer Mercurius was among those papers which furnished material most frequently to the Danish language press. Thus it is hardly surprising that the first version of the Declaration printed in Danish was a translation from the August 23 German-language *Altonaischer Mercurius*. This appeared, as noted, in *Kiøbenhavnske Tidender*, September 2, 1776.

Whatever its reasons, there is no indication that *Kiøbenhavnske Tidender* was in any hurry to publish its translation. If mail delivery on the main route between Hamburg and Copenhagen was normal, the Friday, August 23 edition of *Altonaischer Mercurius* could have arrived in Copenhagen early Monday morning, August 26. So it should have been possible to publish the Danish version, if not on August 26, then at least on August 30 – as happened in Sweden, where *Göteborgs Allehanda* that very day carried a Swedish translation. Like the *Kiøbenhavnske Tidender* edition, this was based on a German version.

This implies no lack of recognition of the Declaration's significance, since when the news finally was broken in Copenhagen, it was on page one as the top news of that day. Ironically, the Declaration appeared under the dateline "London, August 16." *Kiøbenhavnske Tidender* did not advertise the fact that it depended on German language newspapers as a major source of foreign news.

However, there is no doubt that the Danish text *was* translated from *Altonaischer Mercurius,* both because the brief news announcement preceding the Declaration corresponded word for word with the German equivalent, and because a number of details in the Danish version reveal that a German text must have intervened between the American and the Danish. And this was the German text printed in *Altonaischer Mercurius.*

Kiøbenhavnske Tidender's translation, published September 2, 1776, omits the grievances and thus corresponds precisely to what *Altonaischer Mercurius* carried on August 23, 1776. The grievances were not printed separately in a succeeding issue, as they had been in Holstein, but came to light about a month later in the October monthly supplement to *Kiøbenhavnske Tidender* where, as mentioned, the only full (though edited) Danish version appeared. In that version, a number of corrections were made vis-à-vis the September 2 edition, making it probable that, by that time, the original English language text had been made available. Where it came from is impossible to say.

Of all the newspapers in the Danish-speaking parts of Denmark, only *Kiøbenhavnske Tidender* printed the Declaration of Independence. However, America was often mentioned in the other Copenhagen papers and in the then infant Danish provincial press. On Friday, August 30 – just three days before the Copenhagen paper ran its first attenuated version of the manifesto – *Jydske Efterretninger* [The Jutland Bulletin], which still appears in Jutland under the name *Aalborg Stiftstidende* [The Aalborg Times], let it be known that:

"Now the Americans at last shall have taken the step which has long been awaited of them. The General Congress in Philadelphia has declared America an independent state and, in addition, formally declared war on the King, the Lords, the Churches and the People in Great Britain..." (⁸)

As the news of '76 slowly spread in September and October to the Danish reading public (and from there, in more or less original form, most certainly to the taverns and other popular gathering places), so at least some Danes all the way out at the farthest reaches of the kingdom had long since gotten the message. These were the residents of the Danish West Indies (Virgin Islands), for whom North America was quite a different living reality than it was for the rest of the domain. As early as August 17 in the islands' only newspaper,

18

The Royal Danish American Gazette, published in English, the islanders could read a complete and highly accurate version of the Declaration. It was beautifully placed on page one, otherwise reserved for advertising. In the West Indies, far away from the seat of government in Copenhagen, there seemed to be no need for the rewriting and cutting we find in *Kiøbenhavnske Tidender.*

Cette curieuse pièce

From the Danish side, unfortunately, practically no contemporary commentary on the Declaration has come to light. But this was consistent with the policy of Danish newspapers of the day not to editorialize on daily events. In fact, just a single diplomatic dispatch can be cited – to the Department of Foreign Affairs, in Copenhagen, from the Danish chargé d'affaires in London, Frederik von Hanneken. The diplomat, who was old and weak, refers scornfully at the end of his dispatch to the Declaration as *une curieuse pièce,* and cavalierly brushes aside its message as *la frivolité des prétendus raisons.* (9) Hanneken's evaluation clearly reveals a failure to comprehend the contents of the document, but his attitude probably was not far removed from the Danish government's, which was consistent with the view of Americans as enemies of all kings.

For a better impression of how the Declaration was received in Denmark, therefore, one must turn to other sources. The moods manifested toward America and the American cause in those years must be sampled in literature and letters in order to gain some notion of the spirit in which the announcement was received.

In her short story *Sorg-Agre* (Fields of Sorrow), set in Denmark in the 1770s, Karen Blixen (her pen name was Isak Dinesen) brings the dialogue around to America. Adam, a young Danish nobleman and diplomat, sees an old woman on his uncle's estate subjected to treatment that he finds unreasonable and inhuman. In disgust he turns away and determines to leave at once for America:

"I'm going to America, to the New World..." "To America?" says his uncle, raising his eyebrows slightly. "I have heard about America. They have freedom there, a great Waterfall, wild red People. They shoot turkeys in America, I have read, the way we shoot Partridge. Well, if your Mind is set on America, then go there, Nephew. And may you be happy in the New World." (10)

Karen Blixen is not responsible for historical reality, but she undoubtedly hit something central in the temper of the times when she

= ment levé du Gl. Fraser.

Je ne dis rien de la Declaration d'Independance & de Guerre, publiée par les Rebelles, ni de la Frivolité des pretendües Raisons qu'ils y alleguent; la curieuse Pièce étant deja imprimée en toute son insolente Etendüe dans la London Chronicle page 164; Et les divers Gazettiers de la Hollande l'auront deja copiée & traduite.

Sept à 8 Vaisseaux richement chargés sont arrivés de Bengal à la Compe des Indes Orientales, escortés le Quart de leur Route, à sçavoir des Ste. Helene, par un Vaisseau de Guerre.

Plusieurs Vaisseaux de la Flotte Marchande, partie cet Eté des Indes Occidentales, comme l'on appelle icy les isles Caraibes, manquent encore, & les Negocians ont de la Peine d'en trouver des Assureurs à 30 p Cent, & bien au delà. L'Amirauté se flatte pourtant que des Mesures prises par Elle pour garantir cette importante Branche du Comerce Britanique des Entreprises des Rebelles à l'avenir, seront efficaces.

On assure aussi que Vingt Vaisseaux, chargés de toute sorte de Vivres ont deja mis à la Voile de Cork en Irlande vers les dites isles, y obvier à une Famine Generale, & Emûte consecutive des Negres.

Il est arrivé ces jours un Courier de My Lord Grantham, sans doute avec des Depeches relatives à la Dispute entre l'Espagne & le Portugal. Un des Papiers publics qu'on vient m'ap-
= porter

:porter, assure quel. Amb.r d'Espagne setoit rendû à Windsor, & que S. M. B. y avoit conferé avec luy deux heures entieres: Cela est très possible, & de plus probable, mais je n'en ai jusqu'ici aucune autre Certitude que la Foi du Gazetteer.

je viens de recevoir une Circulaire de My Lord Weymouth, qui avertit qu'après demain, (: qui seroit d'ailleurs son jour ordinaire :) Son Exc.e ne sera pas à Loisir de recevoir les Ministres étrangers à son Office. Apparem.t cette Matinée là sera destinée ni à conferer avec l'Amb.r d'Espagnol tout seul, ou à assister à un Conseil sur les Affaires Americaines, peut être à toutes les deux Besognes, à la fois.

J'ai l'honneur d'être avec le plus profond Respect,

Monsieur

de Nôtre Excellence

Londres ce 20 d'Aout
1776.

Le très humble & très obeissant
Serviteur
Hanneken

Last two pages from Frederik von Hanneken's dispatch from London of August 20, 1776. The Royal Archives, Copenhagen. See translation, p. 41.

allowed the young nobleman to entertain the thought of literally and figuratively putting the Old World behind him, and projected the dream of emigrating to America.

Returning to the eighteenth century, there is a personal letter from the Danish Minister of Foreign Affairs, A. P. Bernstorff, to his friend Ditlev Reventlow, who then held the post of curator at the University of Kiel, in Holstein. Dated October 22, 1776, the letter was written in French and contains this passage:

"The public here is extremely occupied with the rebels [in America], not because they know the cause, but because the mania of independence in reality has infected all the spirits, and the poison has spread imperceptibly from the works of the philosophers all the way out to the village schools." ([11])

A pronouncement which falls right in line with what Benjamin Franklin wrote several months later from Paris:

"All Europe is on our Side of the Question, as far as Applause and good Wish can carry them." ([12])

Centered in France, this interest in American affairs developed with explosive speed in the last half of the eighteenth century. By the end of the 1760s it reached Denmark, where a sudden interest can be traced among the educated in works of all kinds dealing with conditions in America. ([13]) At about the same time, Danish newspapers began to make room for American news – found in ever more abundant amounts in the North German press, prime source of foreign news for the Danish papers, as seen from the examples already cited. From 1774-75 onward, American news assumed a dominant place in foreign coverage. And occasionally, Danish newspapers of the day took the most unusual step of breaking up their front pages in order to give American stories top priority, as seen with the Declaration of Independence.

The Danish foreign minister surely was stretching matters with his assertion that *la manie de l'indépendance* had spread out to *les écoles de villages*. Denmark in the 1770s, and long afterward, was a country where the rural population who formed the bulk of society, stood outside the flow of news. Newspapers were published in the towns, principally Copenhagen, and naturally also found most of their readers in these population centers. Town officials, well-placed citizens, students and intellectuals, and – in no small measure – craftsmen and other plain folk, together filled the precincts in which newspaper items circulated and were discussed.

Within these far more limited but still extensive groups, however,

Count Andreas Peter Bernstorff (1735–1797), the Danish Minister of Foreign Affairs. Painting by Jens Juel. The National Historical Museum, Frederiksborg Palace.

Scene from a Copenhagen tavern in the middle 1770s. The reporter is sitting under the table, taking notes. Front page vignette from the Copenhagen newspaper Aftenposten (The Evening Post), September 2, 1776.

it could well be maintained that America in the middle 1770s, when her Declaration reached Denmark, was on everyone's lips, and that the American cause and freedom heroes aroused great if somewhat superficial excitement.

Popular sentiment in Copenhagen

As to the popular mood in the country's largest city, Copenhagen, we are well informed, thanks in great measure to *Aftenposten* [The Evening Post], a paper founded in 1772, whose most active reporter was Emanuel Balling. Through Balling's countless on-the-spot portraits of daily life in the capital, it is clear that the American Revolution and its leaders in 1775-76 entered the conversation in places where average citizens got together:

"To pass the time the other evening, I went to an Ale House, one of our political Schools of Fencing, those bourgeois Art of War Listening Rooms, there, where our little Politici, during a Glass of Ale, a Pinch of Snuff and a Pipe of Tobacco, conclude Alliances, declare Wars, realign States, dethrone Princes, levy Taxes, trade Countries, pass out Offices, and compose the Good of the World..." writes Balling in *Aftenposten*, December 23, 1776, and continues with some samples of the conversation moving around the American Revolution:

"But, said the leader, this General Congress, it's really a plucky Fellow, who holds out so long; he and Washington, they're men. General Philadelphia, said another, he yields them nothing. – Hum! said one, who believed himself to be a little more witty. Philadelphia is really a Town! – No! cried a fourth man, it is a natural person, a real Man, and that I can show by this, that an American traveled around, who made Works of Art, and was named Philadelphia... But, said one, who up to now had not spoken, what about the King in America? – The King! replied another, they really have no King besides him in England! he reigns besides over the American Territory... – Now starts an examination of the Americans' Rights against the English. One said that they were Rebels, and that they ought to be beaten over the Forehead like Bullocks. – One cried that the English ought to be Thrashed. – One said that now the Englishmen had got Something to chew on. – It is an accursed War! said a Sausage stuffer; Rice grain from Carolina now has become so dear, and I am in the Market for white Sausages. – It makes no difference to me about your Sausages, said a Waggoner, if Wood had not become so dear; that Channel is now plugged up, and the Channel in my wheels will soon be the same. Now the Englishman drives the Tar up in the Baltic Sea. – Just as well, said a Swine butcher, then I get a lift for my Fat. – To the Devil both with your white Sausage and your Tar and your Fat, said a Tobacco roller; it makes no difference! As if the Tobacco leaves were not so dear; for the Virginia Trade now is ruined..."

Some of the dialogue well may be ascribed to Balling's good-natured irony, but since the scene as a picture of the times undoubtedly is reliable, it shows there was no lack of real interest or, for that matter, sympathy, for the American cause among this class. It probably was hard to keep the facts straight – who was who, and what was what, on that faraway battlefield – which, of course, led to no misunderstandings about the significance of the war for everyone's own little business.

If we move forward a year from December, 1776, we see in *Aftenposten*, January 12, 1778, that the mania over the American Revolution was still very much alive. A man enters an ale house with the following salute:

"Good evening, Gentlemen! Ha! Ha! Have we the newspapers? Well! What does England say now? They pack it in and ask for the way Home! – Yes! now they run around and pack it in! The Americans shall trick them... – I have heard that the Greenlanders want to ally themselves with the Americans, and when that happens, look Out! How will things look then... Yes, this War will likely make a rather considerable Change in Europe; and should the Americans lose, then the Turks just as well first as last can turn Constantinople over to Russia, and thank Mahommed that they have America to go to..."

Meanwhile, the commentary on America can hardly be called better informed, and people's ignorance about American causes, on which they so freely pass judgement, remains a prime target for Balling's wit. In one place he visits, America's location is the subject of a peppery debate between a soldier and a sailor. (14) The seaman argues that America lies in Turkey. He has sailed through the strait eleven times and ought to know this well.

In a tavern scene the same year (1778), the confusion over America's location and her chances momentarily threatens good relations between Denmark and the United States. A man whose wife lies in childbed sits with a glass of snaps and reads aloud from the newspaper as best he is able – he has forgotten his eyeglasses:

26

"The Ame – – – ricans now stand with – – an Ar – mee of 14 Thousand Men, – – strongly supplied – – with – – a great – – Artillery, and threaten – – – to attack – – us. Us? – Are they mad? The Americans attack us? How the Hell will the black Devils come to Denmark?... No need to fear, though. Why, America lies on the other side of China, and before they get across the Line and come into the North, two-thirds of 'em must be melted. – Yes! that is the truth, too."(15)

Sometimes the appalling misunderstandings, wild speculation, and endless talk gets to be too much for the practical reporter. The gentle irony no longer works, and he falls to moralizing. An argument over whether Howe captured Washington, or Washington Howe, ends with Balling telling off both sides:

"Can what you are quarreling over not be all the same to you? You know just as much about Washington as about Howe. For three Evenings in a row, I have listened with Wonder to your Arguing... can anything be more ridiculous than to neglect one's Concerns at home in order to fight for Hours under some Refreshment of Ale, Aquavit, and Tobacco, over Matters which do not concern us." (16)

But little difference did it seem to make. Ale room speculation over the American Revolution rose to a din all over Europe. (17)

Sentiment among the better situated

If we turn to other, more highly placed groups in Danish society, we do not find such immediately convincing signs of the "America fever" that infected the Copenhagen petite bourgeoisie. Yet the various currents of cultural life give evidence of a growing awareness of American affairs among the better situated. Those who read the newspapers and followed the intellectual currents of the day were, as mentioned, continually confronted with America. Theatergoers had the opportunity to see de Chamfort's sentimental comedy on American themes, "The Young Indian." de Chamfort's play, first performed in 1764 to an America-thrilled Paris, had its Danish premiere in 1776 at The Royal Theater in Copenhagen, where it enjoyed a total of fourteen runs up to the year 1786.

Members of the esteemed and influential Dreier's Club had at their disposal a number of the latest European works on America.(18) Trade in portrait etchings of the American freedom heroes, a typical if very naive example of America worship in France, was also known in Denmark. (19) Publishers also eyed the potential profits in books

Members of the Dreier's Club in the society's reading room. Colored drawing.
The Danish Folkmuseum, Copenhagen.

with American themes for the Danish public, and in these years for the first time, books on America appeared in Danish. First consideration was given to translations of existing works, of which W. Robertson's *History of America* (1780) and Captain John Smith's *Travels* (1783) were the first published.

The established Danish poets, however, did not yet seem to find the time ripe for American themes. On the fringe of the contemporary literature, however, Pastor Søren Møller was a diligent exponent of a genre well known in Germany and France: an almost current-event verse, in which the Americans draw high praise:

"The Folk, who yonder midst Torment and Grief,
have withstood the worst in Winter's Time,
Arise as one out of their Slumber,
And gird themselves anew for Strife,
And double Fieriness from the Spring sun feel,
And Fire and Courage and Strength in the eager Limbs..."

"Yonder, Citizen blood for Citizen runs
on Boston beach midst Scream and Thrust;
And which of Them the Victory wins,
That decides just One, – the great God. –
An advantage they have, though, who for their Freedom fight,
That virtue seems mostly to lie in their Cause." [20]

On the other hand, the British and above all their Hessian hired troops, regularly draw the poet's ire:

"The roaring Horseman and the
hessian Grenadeer,
In his Heart sighs deeply, as soon
as he reflects,
That in alien Causes for Murder
he is hired;
He is like a Machine, which others
must control
Ah, fighting men fight best for
their sweet Home." [21]

Henrik Steffens (1773–1845), author, philosopher, professor. Painting by C. A.
Lorentzen, 1808. Privately owned.

The hearts of the younger sons of the bourgeoisie seemed to beat for the Americans. K. L. Rahbek tells in his memoirs how, as a young man in Copenhagen, one of his dreams was "to go to America as a Militaire." ([22]) And Henrik Steffens, who experienced the American War of Independence from Helsingør (Elsinore), where his father was an esteemed citizen, recalls that:

"There were but few lively young Men in the peace-loving Country [Denmark] who were not Engaged with the cause of the North Americans..." ([23])

And he goes on to say that, so far as he is concerned:

"I was well enough informed about the Significance of the north american War as to be interested with my whole Soul in a People who so bravely fought for their Freedom. Among the greatest Men of the Time, Washington and Franklin stood pre-eminent."

Later, when the romantic reaction took hold, Steffens changed his mind about America and called it:

"...a sad Memorial to a Time,...in which it was believed that States could be constitutionally created." ([24])

Steffens' description of the festivities in Helsingør marking the peace of 1783 really deserves full citation, because it is one of the few firsthand accounts in existence of the ideas about America which moved in that age in a Danish provincial town. How much can be attributed especially to the Declaration of Independence can only be guessed. It is the summation of impressions conveyed by several years' events on the American scene to which the reader here is presented – seen through the spectacles of a keen-eyed observer:

"I still remember quite well the Day of the Peace Treaty which followed the Victory of fighting Freedom, as it happened in Helsingør and in the Harbor. It was a beautiful Day, the Harbor lay full of Ships of all Nations, there were also Warships among them. Already the day before, we had waited with Excitement the dawn of that Morning; all Ships were in their finest Harbor decoration; the Masts were adorned with long Pennants. Not only the Deck Flagstaffs bore the most splendid Flags, the bowsprit also bore one, yes, one saw others between the masts; the brisk Weather gave exactly the right wind to freely unfold the Pennants and the Flags. This unusual decoration, the Cannon salutes from the Warships, yes, from every Merchant Vessel which just had a couple of Cannon; the cheering Crews which filled the Foredecks also made this Day festive for us. Father had invited a couple of Guests and the North Americans' Victory and the cause of Peoples' Freedom was discussed lively, and

"*The Red Building*" *erected 1716–1721. Home of the Department of Foreign Affairs in the 1770s. From Erich Pontoppidan's Danske Atlas (Danish Atlas) of 1764.*

it was probably an Anticipation of the great Events to come out of this victory which filled the Souls of the jubilant People. It was the friendly Dawn of History's bloodiest Days." (25)

"Father wished to nourish this Understanding of civil Liberty in the Boy, how dim and limited it was, or did he have any. We children were called in, much to our surprise, for this was not Customary at that time, to join in the Celebrations of the Grown-ups. Father tried to explain to us the Significance of the festive Day, and when Luck and Success had been drunk for the new Republic, a Danish and a North American Flag were waving in our Garden. A great Fireworks was set off, our glasses were filled with Punch, and we were allowed to be Gay with our Parents, something we indeed did like." (26)

Conservative criticism of America

By no means was there unanimous approval of the American cause among the politically aware segment of the Danish populace. In an autocratic state with a powerful and class-conscious nobility, however, it could hardly be expected that conservative criticism of the American experiment in nation-building should not find a platform. Foreign Minister A. P. Bernstorff's aversion to the colonial "rebels" has already been noted. And as a representative of the state Lutheran Church, Professor Nicolai Balle, later the Bishop of Zealand, in his sermon of November 10, 1776 – just after news of the Declaration had reached Denmark – enjoined in exceedingly sharp phrases the citizen's absolute obligation to the throne, based on Matthew 22, 15-22.

America was not named in the sermon, but it seems safe to presume that Balle was referring to the matter of taxation by drawing a parallel between Matthew 22,21 ("Render therefore to Caesar the things that are Caesar's, and to God the things that are God's") and the Anglo-American conflict, just as it seems likely that he had wanted to raise his voice against the all too widespread sympathy in Denmark for the Americans. (27)

All in all, it would seem that upper-class conservative criticism of the Americans was quite restrained, and that the fronts were not sharply drawn. This probably should be viewed in connection with the fact that the swell of public sympathy for the American cause in its entire character was more superficial, and therefore less threatening to the domestic establishment, than was the case in other European countries, particularly France. It is remarkable that no documents have come to light in Denmark containing more penetrating analyses of the American Revolution with the direct or indirect aim of showing to what extent it could be of concern to Denmark. By contrast to the response abroad, the upheaval unleashed neither revolutionary nor critical currents in Danish intellectual circles.

Why not? One reason might be that Denmark, geographically and culturally, lay on the periphery of Europe, and that personal contacts between the American continent and Denmark in those years were extremely few. Another factor could be the uncertainty over the limits of press freedom. Not knowing what news – or opinion – was fit to print could well have inhibited some from expressing what was in their hearts about America. The gingerly handling of the Declaration of Independence is a case in point.

More decisive, in all probability, was that educated Danes, not without reason, believed that their enlightened monarchy gave Danish society good – indeed enviable – conditions, by comparison with those in the surrounding countries. Neither the influence of American events nor, a few years later, the far more massive influence of events during the French Revolution, managed in any appreciable degree to rock the assumption that Denmark was best served by an absolute monarchy. This in no way implies that the educated classes in Denmark were untouched by the eighteenth century enlightenment. To the contrary, the attitude – and this today would be considered a paradox, even though it was justified in many respects – was that the royal monarchy guaranteed respect for law, property, and personal freedom in a splendid manner. Moreover, people thought that the relatively unrestricted freedom of the press created the groundwork for an informed public political opinion which the government neither could nor wished to ignore. According to this view, Denmark was run, if not by the people, then by an enlightened public opinion. And what the country was not, it could in any case become. The Danish intelligensia only could view the American Revolution with interest and sympathy; but strictly on its own terms, they could see in that war no direct message to Denmark. Political thinking had its premises in the monarchy, and the democratic alternative which America – and soon afterward also France – advanced, and which was a catalyst for political action in other European countries, consequently played no appreciable role for Denmark.

Christiansborg, the residential palace in Copenhagen, erected 1732–1745. Etching by Thura from Hafnia Hodierna, 1748.

This forever memorable day

With the conclusion of the War of Independence, broad public interest in America began to wane and, with the French Revolution in 1789, to meld into this great concluding European event of the eighteenth century.

However, neither the Danish state nor the country's intelligensia could take lightly the new nation struggling to establish itself on the other side of the Atlantic. Regardless of the immediate political situation, America was a fact which demanded attention. And in the years that followed, both the Danish government and educated citizens sought, each in their own way, to come to terms with the emerging great power. The Danish state entered into diplomatic negotiations with the United States, leading in 1801 – only twenty-five years after the signing of the Declaration of Independence – to the establishment of permanent ties between the two countries. (28)

In learned quarters, American studies were expanded and promoted. Scholarly interest developed slowly, it is true. But that importance was attached to the matter seems apparent from the fact that in 1792, in the midst of the French Revolution, when little attention was being paid to America, Copenhagen University announced an essay contest on the subject of "What influence the Discovery of America has had on Humanity in Europe." The two entries stimulated by this competition mark the beginnings of American studies in Denmark, (29) which bore their first independent fruit in 1820 with civil servant C. F. von Schmidt-Phiseldeck's book, *Europa und Amerika, oder die künftige Verhältnisse der civilisirten Welt* [Europe and America, or the future Relations of the civilized World], (Copenhagen, 1820). (30)

Since he was the first Dane to set the Declaration of Independence in world-historical perspective, it seems fair to let von Schmidt-Phiseldeck have the last word in this review of the Declaration and Denmark:

"The fourth of July in the Year 1776 constituted the Opening of a new Period in World History. Not provoked to resistance by the intolerable Oppression of Tyrannical Power, but driven to Rebellion, and embittered by the vital grief of a deeply felt pain over the Arbitrary Interference in their well-earned and until then publicly recognized Rights, the People of the United States of North America on this forever memorable Day declared themselves independent ..." (31)

36

Conrad Georg Friedrich Elias von Schmidt-Phiseldeck (1770–1832), civil servant, political writer. Painting possibly by W. Marstrand. Owned by the family.

References

1. *Kiøbenhavnske Tidender* was founded in 1749. Still published under the name *Berlingske Tidende* [The Berling Times], it is one of Europe's oldest newspapers.
2. The 3,000 figure applies to that part of the circulation reserved for Denmark. In addition, a considerable number of copies went to Norway and Schleswig-Holstein. Here, as everywhere in this book, the dukedoms of Schleswig-Holstein (and Norway) enter the presentation only where their relationship to the subject makes it necessary. This study deals in principle only with the present-day region of Denmark. Circulation figures for Danish newspapers of the 1770s are uncertain. As a basis for the figure quoted, see: F. Olsen, *Postvæsenet i Danmark 1711-1808* [The Postal Service in Denmark, 1711-1808], Copenhagen, 1903, p. 310; Stolpe, *Dagspressen i Danmark, III* [The Daily Press in Denmark, III], Copenhagen, 1881, p. 127 (with source references), and T. Kjærgaard, *En undersøgelse af den offentlige kritik af den danske enevælde 1789-1799* [An Examination of Public Criticism of Danish Absolutism, 1789-1799], Copenhagen, 1973 (unpublished).
3. *Reichs-Post-Reuter*. August 28, 1776.
4. C. L. Becker, *The Declaration of Independence, a Study in the History of Political Ideas*. 1922, p. 18.
5. J. A. Seip, "Teorien om det opinionsstyrte enevelde." ["The Theory of the Opinion–Directed Monarchy."] (Norwegian) *Historisk tidsskrift*, XXXVIII. 1958, pp. 397-464.
6. D. M. Clarc, *British Opinion and the American Revolution*. New Haven/London, 1930, p. 9.
7. *The London Chronicle* published the Declaration of Independence on August 17, 1776.
8. *Jydske Efterretninger* [The Jutland Bulletin], which in the 1770s had an awake and energetic editor in J. P. Wandell, was the first newspaper to publish Thomas Paine in Danish. This was a two-

39

page excerpt entitled, "From the well-known Tract published in Philadelphia: Common Sense." (In a monthly supplement to *Jydske Efterretninger* of September, 1776.) Outside of Aalborg, the towns of Odense and Viborg had their own newspapers.

9. The Royal Archives. Department of Foreign Affairs, 1771-1848. England. Dispatches. Hanneken of London, August 20, 1776. Received in Copenhagen on August 30, 1776.

10. *Vinter-Eventyr*. [Winter Tales.] Copenhagen, 1972, (1942) p. 231.

11. *Bernstorffske Papirer* III. [The Bernstorff Papers III.] Copenhagen, 1913, p. 498.

12. Here cited after H. Koth, *The American Spirit in Europe*. Philadelphia, 1949, p. 14.

13. In the distinguished internationally-oriented periodical, *Kiøbenhavns lærde Efterretninger* [The Copenhagen Informed Bulletin], whose contents reliably reflect the interests of the literary world, only once during the period 1749-1766 – namely in 1752 – was a work on an American subject discussed. Thereafter the picture quickly changed, and up through the 1770s there were many, often highly profound, reviews of works on American themes nearly every year.

14. *Aftenposten*. [The Evening Post.] February 13, 1778.

15. *Aftenposten*. [The Evening Post.] January 30, 1778.

16. *Aftenposten*. [The Evening Post.] February 16, 1778.

17. Cf. Goethe's youth drama *Die Mitschuldigen*, Act 1, Scene 1:
"Well, over a glass of wine I have heard
many a person boast
that he would do everything for my
provincialists*
There, freedom was enthroned,
all were bold and brave.
When morning came he didn't lift a finger."

18. *Catalogus over Bogsamlingen i Klubben af 1775*. [Catalogue of the Book Collection of the Club in 1775.] Dreiers Klub. Copenhagen, 1792.

19. *Luxdorphs Dagbøger*, II. [Luxdorph's Diaries, II.] Copenhagen, 1925, p. 407.

20. *Paketbaaden*, No. 6. April, 1777.

21. *Nye maanedlig Skiald-Tidender*. [New Monthly Skiald-Times.] October, 1776.

* i. e. the Americans.

22. K. L. Rahbek. *Erindringer af mit Liv* I. [Memories of My Life, I.] Copenhagen, 1824, p. 356. He frankly acknowledges that he might have been motivated by the desire to experience the adventure of military service more than to aid the Americans.

23. H. Steffens. *Was ich erlebte* I. [My Experiences, I.] Breslau, 1841, p. 78.

24. H. Steffens. *Die gegenwärtige Zeit und wie sie geworden* II. [The Contemporary Period and How it was Created, II.] Berlin, 1817, p. 330.

25. A reference to the French Revolution.

26. H. Steffens. *Was ich erlebte,* pp. 79-81.

27. N. Balle. *Christi Læres herlige Indflydelse paa det borgerlige Livs Sikkerhed og Velfærd.* [The Glorious Influence of Christian Learning on the Security and Welfare of Civil Life.] Copenhagen, 1776.

28. Government relations between the United States and Denmark, which fall outside the scope of this book, are treated in S.J.M.P. Fogdall, *Danish-American Diplomacy 1776-1920,* Iowa, 1922, and by O. Feldbæk, *Dansk neutralitetspolitik under krigen 1778-83.* [The Danish Policy of Neutrality During the War 1778-1783.] Copenhagen, 1971. (English summary).

29. The authors were E. Christian von Haven and A. P. Meden. Only the first work was printed. Also noteworthy is N. C. Claussens book, *Undersøgelse om Amerikas opdagelse har mere skadet end gavnet det menneskelige Kiøn* [An Investigation of whether the Discovery of America has Hurt More than Helped the Human Race], Copenhagen, 1785. This was the first book written by a Dane about America.

30. Translated in the following years into five languages, including English. (1820).

31. *Europa und Amerika,* p. 11.

Frederik von Hanneken's dispatch from London (partial translation from the original French, pp. 20–21): I shall say nothing of the Declaration of Independence and of War, which the rebels have published, nor of the levity of the reasons set out therein, since this peculiar document has already been printed in its insolent entirety on page 164 of the London Chronicle and the various gazetteers in Holland have already copied and translated it.

Seven or eight richly loaded vessels have arrived from Bengal for the East India Company under the escort of a man-of-war for one fourth of their voyage, namely from Saint Helena.

Several vessels of the merchant marine which have departed this summer from the West Indies – as the Caribbean Isles are called here – are still missing, and merchants have difficulty finding under-writers at premiums of 30 per cent or more. The Admiralty, however, prides itself on the effective measures it has taken to protect this important branch of British trade against any future encroachment by the rebels.

Assurances have also been given that 20 vessels carrying all kinds of victuals have already set sail from Cork in Ireland for the said Isles in order to obviate a general famine there and a resultant uprising by the Negroes.

Within the last few days a courier has arrived from My lord Gresham, undoubtedly with dispatches about the dispute between Spain and Portugal. According to one of the papers I have just received, the Ambassador of Spain yesterday presented himself at Windsor where His Britannic Majesty conferred with him for two full hours. This may indeed and very likely be so, but I have only the gazetteer's word for it.

I have just received a circular from Lord Weymouth, advising me that on the day after tomorrow (which would ordinarily be his day for visitors) it will not be His Excellency's pleasure to receive the ministers of foreign nationality. Apparently that morning will be set aside for a conference with the Spanish Ambassador alone or for attendance at a council on the American affairs, or perhaps both at the same time.

I have the honour to remain most respectfully,

Your Excellency's
Most Humble and Obedient Servant

(Hanneken)
London, August 20th, 1776

42

The author: Thorkild Kjærgaard was born in Nørre Felding in 1945. He studied history at Copenhagen University, where he is working as a postgraduate fellow.

Published by the Danish Bicentennial Committee to commemorate the 200th Anniversary of the American Revolution.
This complimentary book is printed in an edition of 6,000 copies.

Produced by the Royal Danish Ministry of Foreign Affairs, Press and Cultural Relations Department, Christiansborg Palace, DK 1218 Copenhagen K, Denmark.

Editor: Ole Kjær Madsen
Translator: Fradley Garner
Art Director: Knud Rath
Printer: Bonde's Bogtryk/offset, Copenhagen
ISBN 8785112232